CONTENTS

multi-agency working:
an audit of activity

Mary Atkinson
Anne Wilkin
Alison Stott
Kay Kinder

Local Government Association

INVESTOR IN PEOPLE

nfer

Published in February 2001
by the National Foundation for Educational Research,
The Mere, Upton Park, Slough, Berkshire SL1 2DQ

ISBN 1 903880 00 9

ACKNOWLEDGEMENTS

The authors would like to thank all the LEA personnel who completed pro formas and gave up their time to take part in the telephone interviews which provided valuable data for this phase of the study.

We are particularly grateful to Michelle Robinson, Jenny Price and Phil Craig for reading and commenting on the early drafts of this report. We would also like to thank our colleagues at NFER: Sandra Brown, for acting as our internal reader; David Upton, for editorial input; and lastly, Hilary McElderry, Sally Wilson and Sue Medd, for providing secretarial support.

INTRODUCTION

As part of the Government's current agenda of social inclusion, multi-agency approaches and activity have been given much prominence. From many different sources (e.g. the Social Exclusion Unit's reports; the Audit Commission; DfEE initiatives, such as New Start; Standards Fund criteria; Behaviour Support Plans and Education Development Plans), the desirability – and indeed necessity – for Education Services to work with other local authority agencies is made clear. Equally, Health Trusts and Social Services have their own planning imperatives and targets that clearly require collaboration and coordination with their local authority colleagues in Education. It is often stated that such coordination will ensure each service's 'clients' (e.g. young people 'at risk'; or those with special needs) are provided with a more coherent support system, preventing duplication or omission, and that services themselves would benefit from this more effective and cost-effective approach. At the same time, LEA services such as Youth, Leisure and Community are also being included in mainstream educational activity and initiatives in a number of innovative ways (e.g. in relation to arts and cultural opportunities, learning support out of school hours, and information and communications technology) and these may be addressing the whole 'achievement' agenda in a newly coherent way.

Notwithstanding this, in the multi-agency activity undertaken thus far, accounts of initial problems (such as confidentiality and information exchange) and different professional cultures (with different expectations of the client group) have emerged at operational level, as well as issues at strategic level, such as lack of time and structural inflexibility at strategic level. Despite this, examples of successful joint projects, initiatives and strategic activity, particularly with regard to young people at risk of social exclusion, are in evidence in a number of recent research and evaluation reports, and it is these successes which are likely to provide useful material for further research. To date, much recent research has focused on the impact of such initiatives on the young people themselves, at least as much as the professional processes of collaboration and joint working. This project, however, gives particular attention to the professionals themselves – at both strategic and operational level. It aims to explore the key factors in successful coordination of inter-service activity and the impact of such collaboration on the professionals themselves and their own agencies.

Aims

The overall study endeavours to:

- ◆ **identify and audit a range of different examples of coordinated and multi-agency activity between Health and/ or Social Services and LEA providers**

- ◆ **adumbrate key factors in the perceived success of these collaborations and, equally, any inhibiting factors**

- ◆ **provide an in-depth and evaluative review of the impact of such joint working on the practice of professionals and their service.**

Methodology

The research consists of three phases, and it is the purpose of this interim report to present the findings of Phase One of the study.

Phase One of the study consisted of an initial audit of multi-agency approaches using a well-tried informal survey approach. At the beginning of the summer term 2000, pro formas were sent to all LEAs, encouraging them to identify examples of innovative and effective practice in the area of inter-service coordination and collaboration. They were asked, if possible, to highlight three examples of effective collaborative working practice, one involving Social Services and Education, one involving Health and Education and one involving all three of these agencies. LEA personnel were asked to specify a named contact for each area of practice they identified, and these were followed up with telephone interviews with all contacts within responding LEAs. Within the telephone interviews, the following areas of information were covered:

- the agencies involved

- the area of education and target group

- the rationale for a coordinated approach

- a brief description of service delivery

- the benefits and challenges associated with the initiatives

- the key factors in the success of initiatives.

The report

The first part of the report provides an overall audit of multi-agency activity: the background and rationale for the initiatives, the focus of the work and the agencies that were involved. The second part of the report moves on to present the benefits and challenges associated with multi-agency work, as identified by interviewees, and the key factors which were thought to be associated with the success of the initiatives highlighted. The study sample proved to be representative of LEAs nationally, in terms of size and type of LEA, i.e. county, London borough, etc., and further details of the sample characteristics can be found in Appendix 1.

In total, 117 LEAs responded and 149 LEA personnel were interviewed. The interviewees included, in rank order, heads of service or service managers (53), education officers (25) assistant directors (20), directors (10), Educational Psychologists (10), advisers or inspectors (9) and project coordinators or managers (9), whilst the remainder (13) included a variety of personnel, including team leaders and Principal Education Welfare Officers (called Principal Education Social Workers in some LEAs).

It is important to note that at this stage of the research, data collected on the specific Education services involved in the initiatives was limited, and this will be explored in more detail in Phases Two and Three of the study.

PART 1. AN AUDIT OF MULTI-AGENCY ACTIVITY

Introduction

This chapter focuses on an overall audit of the multi-agency activity highlighted within the telephone interviews with personnel from the 117 LEAs who returned initial pro formas. LEA personnel were asked to identify initiatives that they considered to be examples of effective collaborative working between Social Services, Health and Education, Social Services and Education or Health and Education. They were encouraged to highlight one example within each of these categories. Overall, a total of 221 initiatives were identified, and these were followed up with telephone interviews. This chapter focuses on the following areas, which were discussed within the telephone interviews:

- the background and rationale behind each initiative
- the focus or target group
- the agencies involved.

1.1 Background and rationale

During the telephone interviews, interviewees were asked to briefly describe the background to, and history of, the initiative. Interviewees were specifically asked to consider the main rationale for the foundation of the initiative, and give details of any local and national factors or issues which were influential during its formation.

Fundamental rationale for the development of multi-agency initiatives

Part of the discussion about the background to the different multi-agency initiatives involved the examination of the different initial reasons and motivation for setting up such initiatives. Responses were often coded into more than one category, and Table 1.1 summarises the most frequent responses.

Table 1.1 shows the most commonly given reasons for forming multi-agency initiatives, but also highlights notable differences between initiatives involving different agencies.

From this table, it can be seen that, in general, the main rationale for setting up a multi-agency initiative was the needs of a specific target group (looked-after children (LAC), disaffected children, or those with special needs, for example) – whether locally or nationally identified. This was particularly the case for initiatives involving Health and Education, and least commonly mentioned for initiatives involving all three agencies.

Table 1.1   Rationale for the development of multi-agency initiatives. Factors mentioned by interviewees from ten per cent, or more, of the total sample of 221 initiatives

Reasons for development	Social Services, Health and Education		Social Services and Education		Health and Education		TOTAL	
	No.	% N=107	No.	% N=64	No.	% N=50	No.	% N=221
Target group – locally or nationally identified need	23	21	19	30	23	46	**65**	**29**
Response to Government trend/initiative	18	17	21	33	8	16	**47**	**21**
A specific desire for multi-agency working	18	17	9	14	11	22	**38**	**17**
Desire for comprehensive/ effective service provision	24	22	7	11	4	8	**35**	**16**
Overlap of departments work/target groups	20	19	4	6	4	8	**28**	**13**
A funding bid/meeting funding criteria	9	8	7	11	6	12	**22**	**10**
Response to review/research	8	7	9	14	4	8	**21**	**10**

Interviewees were able to give more than one response, and therefore percentages do not sum to 100 per cent.
Source: Telephone interviews in Phase One of the NFER study, 2000.

The second most commonly given reason was in response to a Government agenda or directive – again, often involving a specific target group. This was most frequently mentioned by interviewees from initiatives between Social Services and Education – and was the most commonly cited of all the factors for this group. Government agendas mentioned included, among others, social inclusion, raising the attainment of LAC, and the focus on joined-up thinking and multi-agency working. These agendas are discussed in more detail in the section dealing specifically with national influences.

The next three items on the list relate to the provision of an effective service – particularly in situations where the target groups' needs and the agencies' activities overlapped. This was often simply noted as a desire to work more closely together, and was also frequently associated with initiatives involving all three agencies in strategic planning functions.

Other reasons for establishing multi-agency initiatives, mentioned by less than ten per cent of the total sample, included: the need for strategic planning or funding protocols, the need for local professionals to share information, and building on other local or national projects.

A range of illustrative examples of the different types of rationale for establishing multi-agency initiatives described by interviewees is shown on the following page.

Examples of main rationales behind multi-agency initiatives

Target group – locally or nationally identified need	One initiative was formed following local government reorganisation in 1997. At the time, high numbers of secondary school pupils in Years 9 and 10 were being excluded. Research showed that many of these pupils were known to the different services since the age of seven or eight, and it was therefore decided that a multi-agency approach to early intervention involving Social Services and Education would be the most beneficial for this group. Another authority had identified a significant increase in the numbers of autistic children in the authority, and therefore needed to increase the capacity of provision. The problem was recognised by all three key agencies (Social Services, Health and Education) and was therefore addressed using a multi-agency approach.
Response to Government trend/initiative	In Wales, the National Assembly set a target for LEAs to increase the educational attainment of LAC. In response, one authority had considered the issue in their area and recognised that they could not always identify the LAC. As a result, they formed a children's support group between Social Services and Education in order to develop shared information systems and support strategies.
A specific desire for multi-agency working	One of the interviewees described the desire to address the needs of LAC in the area in a multi-agency way in order to consider the total needs of the child, rather than specific agency-related needs. This resulted in the formation of a new department – 'Children's Services' incorporating Social Services and Education, and allowing them to work much more closely together. In another authority, an interviewee described the desire for more closely integrated working between Social Services, Health and Education in order to help each individual agency meet their planning requirements. Previously, each of the key agencies had to develop various 'plans', but now there was a clear vision in the area of having one totally integrated 'plan' for the authority.
Desire for comprehensive/ effective service provision	Following local government reorganisation, one new unitary authority decided that joint working between Social Services, Health and Education was required in order to provide a comprehensive and effective service for children with special needs. The main aim was to provide a seamless, transparent service which provided adequate information for parents and avoided cases being passed from one agency to another.
Overlap of departments' work/target groups	In many cases multi-agency working was established as a response to an identified overlap of agencies' work, or target groups. This was the case in one authority where the senior managers of the three key agencies (Social Services, Health and Education) recognised that they were often dealing with the same children (with special needs). Services were poorly coordinated and fragmented, and individual agencies were often unaware of each other's interventions. The initiative was set up to facilitate the sharing of information and a more coordinated approach.
A funding bid/ meeting funding criteria	In one area, the Health Authority invited bids for money to conduct a health promotion project. The Education Department submitted a bid to develop an educational strand for the Child and Adolescent Mental Health Service (CAMHS) strategy. At the same time, similar bids were submitted by other agencies and voluntary groups. In response to these similar bids, the Health Authority asked the various groups to work together in developing one joint project. In several cases, the initiative was based on development work which had been done for a funding bid which was then unsuccessful. One authority had done a lot of work in developing a Standards Fund bid for a speech and language project. Despite the failure of the bid, money from Health was already earmarked, and it was decided to proceed with the project anyway.
Response to review/ research	A large county authority had conducted a review of the entire authority organisation, including a thorough review of all the services provided. Following the initial review, a considerable consultation programme was undertaken. The review and consultation had led to development in the organisational structure of the authority and the services provided by Social Services, Health and Education – changes which were now in the process of being implemented.

Source: Telephone interviews in Phase One of the NFER study, 2000.

Local influences

In addition to the main rationale for developing initiatives, various factors were identified as influencing the initiatives at a local level. Table 1.2 shows the different local influences mentioned and the variation between collaborations involving different agencies.

Table 1.2 **Local influences on the development of multi-agency initiatives. Factors mentioned by interviewees from ten per cent, or more, of the total sample of 221 initiatives**

Local influences	Social Services, Health and Education		Social Services and Education		Health and Education		TOTAL	
	No.	% N=107	No.	% N=64	No.	% N=50	No.	% N=221
Target group characteristics locally	24	22	26	41	15	30	**65**	**29**
A shortage or lack of current provision	15	14	7	11	10	20	**32**	**14**
A history of multi-agency working in the authority	20	19	2	3	7	14	**29**	**13**
A local review of services or research	11	10	8	13	9	18	**28**	**13**
Experience, commitment or interest of staff	12	11	11	17	5	10	**28**	**13**
Local government reorganisation	17	16	5	8	6	12	**28**	**13**

Interviewees were able to give more than one response, and therefore percentages do not sum to 100 per cent.
Source: Telephone interviews in Phase One of the NFER study, 2000.

The table shows that, in agreement with the fundamental rationale for establishing multi-agency collaboration, the characteristics of the target group were the key factor influencing the initiatives at a local level. This was often closely associated with a shortage, or complete lack, of provision – often specifically for the identified target group.

Thirteen per cent of the total sample referred to the importance of a history of close relationships or multi-agency working within the authority in the past as a factor influencing the current initiative. However, only three per cent of interviewees from initiatives involving Social Services and Education mentioned this factor.

The past experience, interest or commitment of particular members of staff within the initiatives were often identified as sources of considerable influence. This was particularly the case in initiatives involving Social Services and Education – mentioned by 17 per cent of the interviewees compared with 13 per cent of the total sample.

Local government reorganisation was an issue raised particularly by interviewees from initiatives involving all three agencies – 17 out of the 27 interviewees who mentioned this factor were from this type of initiative. Four of the interviewees came from Welsh authorities, 19 were from new city authorities, and four were from new regional authorities. Interviewees often described the reorganisation as an opportunity to '*start again*'.

Other local influences, mentioned by less than ten per cent of the sample, included: local consultation, the size and boundaries of the authority and other successful projects – both locally and nationally.

The following chart provides illustrations of the local factors influencing multi-agency initiatives, as highlighted by interviewees.

Examples of local factors identified by interviewees

Target group characteristics locally	One authority identified a significant increase in the numbers of children with speech and learning difficulties. This was seen to be putting pressure on specialist services. As a result, it was decided to try to address these problems earlier and provide children with maximum access to inclusive education. This was achieved through an initiative between Health, Education and a voluntary organisation providing support within nursery provision. Another area faced particular problems because of the small pockets of deprivation within a generally wealthy population. Targeting the pockets of need was a problem, but there were also issues relating to the emotional and psychiatric difficulties associated with affluence, such as high levels of family breakdown. The CAMHS strategy which was implemented, involving Social Services, Health and Education, was set up to consider these issues.
A shortage or lack of current provision	Through local consultation as part of the Behaviour Support Plan it was identified, in one authority, that there was no primary-level behaviour support. The schools in the consultation said that this was something they would welcome, in addition to Educational Psychology Services. As a result, a multi-disciplinary Primary Behaviour Support Team was formed.
A history of multi-agency working in the authority	An interviewee from a small unitary authority thought that this was a very significant factor in developing their multi-agency Behaviour Resource Service. Close working relationships between the agencies already existed and there was considerable trust between them. No rigid boundaries were being created, and there was already a clear corporate voice and a sense of everyone working together to support young people.
A local review of services or research	As part of a local review of services for children with special needs, parent conferences were held. At one of these conferences, parents raised the issue of Attention Deficit Hyperactivity Disorder (ADHD), angry that their children had previously been classified as EBD or 'bad'. It was decided to arrange a meeting specifically to address this issue – 50 people turned up. This provided the impetus to form a multi-agency team to tackle issues relating to pupils with ADHD.
Experience, commitment or interest of staff	A multi-agency initiative addressing the requirements of the UN convention on the rights of the child was influenced considerably by the staff involved at local level, according to one interviewee. Several key managers had been recruited from other authorities, and it was clear that they were very committed to the issue of children's rights, and brought with them fresh ideas and good practices from their previous positions.
Local government reorganisation	The formation of new unitary authorities as part of the local government reorganisation often influenced the formation of multi-agency initiatives. In one case, the reorganisation provided new opportunities to develop better collaborative working arrangements, and provided a more comprehensive service for disaffected children.

Source: Telephone interviews in Phase One of the NFER study, 2000.

National influences

In addition to the local influences on multi-agency initiative formation, interviewees referred to a considerable number of different national influences, including Government agendas and directives. However, only four were mentioned by more than ten per cent of the total sample. Table 1.3 summarises the factors mentioned by more than five per cent of the total sample:

Table 1.3 **National influences on the development of multi-agency initiatives. Factors mentioned by interviewees from five per cent, or more, of the total sample of 221 initiatives**

National influences	Social Services, Health and Education		Social Services and Education		Health and Education		TOTAL	
	No.	% N=107	No.	% N=64	No.	% N=50	No.	% N=221
Quality Protects	12	11	25	39	0	0	**37**	**17**
Government demands for joined-up thinking	18	17	5	8	4	8	**27**	**12**
Social inclusion agenda	8	7	13	20	4	8	**25**	**11**
LAC agenda	4	4	19	30	0	0	**23**	**10**
The Children's Services Plan	11	10	2	3	2	4	**15**	**7**
Work/projects in other authorities	5	5	4	6	1	2	**10**	**5**
Standards Fund	2	2	4	6	4	8	**10**	**5**
Sure Start initiative	10	9	0	0	0	0	**10**	**5**

Interviewees were able to give more than one response, and therefore percentages do not sum to 100 per cent.
Source: Telephone interviews in Phase One of the NFER study, 2000.

The 'Quality Protects' documentation – specifically addressing the needs of LAC – is clearly felt to be the most influential Government directive in terms of multi-agency working. Not surprisingly, this was a factor apparent, on the whole, for initiatives involving Social Services and Education – 21 of the 25 comments being made by interviewees from initiatives set up to address problems for LAC.

The general Government focus on the needs of LAC, and the social inclusion agenda, were clearly also apparent as national influences on multi-agency initiatives – most commonly mentioned by those involving Social Services and Education, or less commonly, all three agencies. Within the table, specific references to 'Quality Protects' were coded as such, and more general references to the needs of looked-after children (which did not specifically mention 'Quality Protects') were coded separately, although it is recognised that there is a considerable level of overlap between these two categories.

Twenty-seven interviewees (12 per cent of the total sample) described Government 'pressure' on local authorities to increase levels of multi-agency working and joined-up thinking. As expected, this was mentioned most frequently by interviewees from initiatives involving all three main agencies, rather than Health and Education, or Social Services and Education.

Other factors mentioned by less than five per cent of the total sample included: the Behaviour Support Plan (BSP), the 'Connexions' initiative, the Early Years Development and Childcare Partnership (EYDCP) and the general theme of raising educational attainment.

The Healthy Schools Initiative was the national influence cited most frequently by interviewees from collaborations involving Health and Education. It was mentioned by 14 per cent of interviewees from these initiatives. However, it does not appear on the table because it was mentioned by only four per cent of the total sample. In addition, it can be seen from Table 1.3 that interviewees from Health and Education collaborations made few (if any) references to the initiatives included in the table – clearly highlighting the differences between initiatives involving different partners.

1.2 The focus or target group

Interviewees were asked to specify the target group or focus for the initiative. A wide range of target groups/focuses was identified. As indicated in the previous section, many initiatives were targeted at specific groups of children, for example LAC and those with special educational needs (SEN), whilst others had a broader focus, such as health improvement or strategic planning. The focus for the initiatives highlighted included:

♦ **Looked-after children**

These initiatives were focused on the needs of children within the care of the local authority.

♦ **Disaffected pupils**

These initiatives were targeted at pupils described by interviewees as disengaged from the education system, either through lack of attendance at school or through exclusion.

♦ **Pupils with SEN**

This group of initiatives included both those focused on all SEN pupils generally and those with a more specific target group, such as children with autism, ADHD, hearing impairment, learning difficulties or physical disabilities.

- **Pupils with speech and language difficulties**

  Whilst also recognised as a special educational need, initiatives focused on children with speech and language difficulties were retained as a discrete group because of the large number of initiatives identified by interviewees and their specific characteristics.

- **Pupils with complex needs**

  As interviewees indicated, this group of initiatives concentrated on pupils whose needs were such that they required a range of interventions, often from Social Services, Health, as well as Education. Whilst initiatives often dealt with a large number of pupils with SEN, they also included some pupils who fell outside this remit and who required therapeutic and care input as well as additional education support.

- **Children with mental health problems**

  In some cases, these initiatives were reported to be targeted at parents with mental health problems, as well as their children.

- **Children in need or at risk**

  This group of initiatives included those focused on 'children in need' as defined by the Children Act 1989, as well as those children felt to be at risk or in need of protection, such as young people involved in prostitution.

- **Early years**

  These initiatives were centred on provision for children between the ages of 0–5 years and their parents.

- **Counselling, advice and mentoring for pupils**

  Whilst not focused on the needs of a specific target group, the main feature within these initiatives was the support provided for pupils with problems, and they took the form of either counselling, information and advice services for young people or mentoring programmes.

- **Health improvement**

  Whilst again not focused on a specific target group, the common feature of these initiatives was that they aimed to promote and improve the health of all children of school age. Some were reported to be focused on whole-school health improvement, as in the Government's Healthy Schools Initiative (mentioned previously), whilst others were focused on more specific areas of health improvement or specific curriculum areas, such as drug education.

- **Strategic planning**

  Initiatives which involved strategic planning included those focused on the planning and development of services. They had a broad remit, such as addressing issues around planning for all services for children and young people, but no specific focus or target group was specified by interviewees.

Detailed illustrations of initiatives within each of the target groups are provided at the end of this chapter.

Table 1.4 shows the number of different initiatives identified within each target group, in rank order, together with their percentages.

Table 1.4   Classification of initiatives by target group or focus

Target group/focus	Number of initiatives	Percentage (N=221)
Looked-after children	46	21
Pupils with SEN	28	13
Health improvement	25	11
Strategic planning	21	10
Disaffected pupils	19	9
Pupils with complex needs	18	8
Children with mental health problems	15	7
Children in need or at risk	15	7
Pupils with speech and language difficulties	14	6
Early years	14	6
Counselling, advice and mentoring for pupils	6	3

All percentages have been rounded to the nearest whole number, and therefore may not add up to 100.
Source: Telephone interviews in Phase One of the NFER study, 2000.

Overwhelmingly, LAC formed the largest target group, with over a fifth of all the initiatives identified focused on this area, perhaps reflecting the Government emphasis on the needs of this vulnerable group through Quality Protects, as discussed earlier. Whilst initiatives focused on pupils with SEN formed the next largest group, when taken together with those targeted at pupils with speech and language difficulties, they comprised 42 initiatives (just under a fifth of all the initiatives). Overall, therefore, initiatives focused on pupils with SEN included 15 that were targeted at all SEN pupils, 14 solely focused on pupils with speech and language difficulties and 13 initiatives focused on pupils with other specific special educational needs, such as autism (4), ADHD (2), learning difficulties (2), hearing impairment (1) and physical disabilities (4). In addition, 18 initiatives were identified as addressing the difficulties of pupils with complex needs. Health improvement and strategic planning each formed the focus of over a tenth of all the initiatives. In contrast, initiatives focused on other areas, such as disaffected pupils, pupils with mental health problems, children in need or at risk, and early years work were highlighted by less than one-tenth of all the interviewees, despite Government requirements for the formation of

Early Years and Childcare Development Partnerships. Finally, initiatives involving counselling, advice and mentoring provision for children formed a particularly small group of multi-agency initiatives.

When examining the different LEAs within which personnel chose to highlight initiatives with certain focuses, it was found that multi-agency work within initiatives concerning LAC, although also conducted within new city and new regional LEAs, tended to be highlighted by interviewees mainly within the London boroughs and metropolitan authorities. With high levels of deprivation, there is likely to be a greater number of such vulnerable children concentrated in these areas, perhaps making the need to target them more pressing. On the other hand, work focused on pupils with SEN was identified more by personnel from London boroughs, new city authorities and, notably, a large number of Welsh authorities, perhaps reflecting a particular drive in these areas at the present time. In addition, initiatives focused on children and families with mental health problems and health improvement tended to be highlighted mainly within the large authorities (metropolitan and new regional authorities in the latter and both these and county authorities in the former). Strategic planning initiatives, in contrast, were identified in a large number of county LEAs and new city authorities. As interviewees highlighted, local government reorganisation frequently presented an ideal opportunity for getting agencies together at strategic level for the purposes of planning and development (a point also raised previously when discussing the local factors influencing multi-agency work). Multi-agency initiatives focused on LAC, pupils with complex needs and children in need tended to be identified by large and medium-sized authorities rather than small ones, whereas initiatives with pupils with SEN and disaffected pupils as their target groups tended to be equally identified by small, medium and large LEAs.

1.3 The agencies involved

Interviewees were asked to identify the different agencies involved in the initiatives that they had highlighted. Initiatives were then grouped according to whether they involved, in the main, all three agencies, Social Services and Education or Health and Education, and the numbers of these are shown in Table 1.5. In the two latter groups, there were some cases where interviewees indicated that there was some, but minimal, involvement of the other agency. In such cases, the initiative was classified according to the two agencies predominantly involved.

Almost half of all the initiatives identified involved all three of the main agencies, whilst just under a third involved Social Services and Education and just under a quarter involved Health and Education. In addition, interviewees noted that other agencies were also involved. Just under a fifth of the initiatives (41), for example, also were reported to involve the voluntary sector, whilst about a tenth of interviewees (23) stated that the initiatives involved a range of other agencies, including the police, probation, the Careers Service, etc.

Table 1.5 The number and percentage of initiatives within each target group involving different agencies, as identified by interviewees

Target group/focus	Social Services, Health and Education		Social Services and Education		Health and Education	
	No. N=107	%	No. N=64	%	No. N=50	%
Looked-after children	9	8	37	58	0	0
Pupils with SEN	17	16	3	5	8	16
Health improvement	3	3	0	0	22	44
Strategic planning	16	15	5	8	0	0
Disaffected pupils	8	7	11	17	0	0
Pupils with complex needs	17	16	1	2	0	0
Children with mental health problems	11	10	0	0	4	8
Children in need or at risk	9	8	4	6	2	4
Pupils with speech and language difficulties	1	1	0	0	13	26
Early years	13	12	1	2	0	0
Counselling, advice and mentoring for pupils	3	3	2	3	1	2

All percentages have been rounded to the nearest whole number, and therefore may not add up to 100.
Source: Telephone interviews in Phase One of the NFER study, 2000.

As can be seen from Table 1.5, within five of the target groups on which initiatives were focused, the majority of initiatives involved **all three of the main agencies**. This included those focused on pupils with complex needs, where, as indicated by interviewees, the diverse needs of the target group suggested the necessity for the involvement of a range of agencies. It also included the initiatives focused on strategic planning, reflecting the overlapping of areas of work within in all three agencies at strategic level and emphasis presently placed by the Government on joint planning and working together at strategic level. Initiatives focusing on early years work, on the other hand, were commonly seen to involve all three key agencies, suggesting a move within all three agencies to adopt a more preventative approach and to tackle problems early, as well as Government imperatives for joint working within this field. Over half the initiatives targeted at SEN pupils also involved all three of the main agencies, but these tended to be those focused broadly on a wide range of SEN rather than those with specific needs, which included a lot of Health and Education initiatives, reflecting the large number of these children with health, as well as educational needs. Mental health, recently highlighted by the Government, also featured mainly professionals from all three agencies. In addition, there was a strong voluntary sector involvement in some of these areas, for example, in six initiatives focused on SEN pupils, six 'early years' initiatives and four with a mental health focus.

Initiatives involving **Social Services and Education** focused mainly on addressing the needs of LAC, with over half of all of them falling within this category. They also featured highly in the area of disaffection with almost a fifth within this group. This suggests recognition of the requirement to address the needs of this challenging group of pupils in a holistic manner and to address their social as well as their educational needs in order to make an impact. Despite the recognition of the link between mental health problems and disaffected pupils made by some interviewees, lack of health involvement in these areas was notable, although a number of other agencies were also mentioned in connection with work with disaffected pupils, e.g. the police and the Careers Service. Voluntary sector involvement also appeared to be a key factor in the work focused on LAC, and was highlighted in eight of these initiatives.

Over a third of the initiatives involving Social Services and Education also involved other agencies. Half of these (13) involved a voluntary agency, whilst half (13) also involved health to some extent (although insufficiently to be classified as an initiative involving all three agencies, according to interviewees), and their involvement was often at a strategic level only. Other agencies cited included the police (2), the Careers Service (2), training providers (1) and Youth Offending Teams (1), and the remainder were reported to each involve a whole range of other agencies.

Joint work involving **Health and Education** was focused mainly on the general health improvement of children within schools or on the needs of children with specific SEN, such as those with speech and language difficulties, ADHD, autism or hearing impairment. Initiatives focused on general health improvement were reported also to entail the involvement of a range of other agencies, including the police and the voluntary sector.

Overall, about a third of the initiatives (15 out of the 50) that involved Health and Education also involved other agencies. Of these 15 initiatives, five involved voluntary agencies, four involved the police and four involved Social Services (although insufficiently to be classified as an initiative involving all three of the main agencies, according to interviewees). Four were also cited as involving a whole range of other agencies, whilst one involved a university and another an agency from the private sector.

When examining the LEAs in which personnel highlighted the work of different agencies, the following points were noted. Initiatives involving multi-agency work between Health and Education and Social Services and Education were mainly identified by new city, new regional LEAs and London boroughs, whereas initiatives involving all three agencies were identified equally within authorities of all different types. Initiatives from within all three categories showed the same pattern in that most were highlighted within large LEAs, slightly less within medium-sized authorities and even fewer within small authorities.

Summary

Background and rationale

A variety of different reasons were given by interviewees for the initial development of multi-agency initiatives. In addition, a number of local and national factors and influences were also cited. In summary:

- The needs of the target group (coupled with their local and national characteristics) were the most common rationale for setting up a multi-agency initiative. The target group also appeared to be closely linked to the choice of partner agencies within the initiative, and the Government agendas and directives which were taken into account.

- Responding to Government agendas and directives was another common reason for establishing a multi-agency initiative. A wide range of different national themes and documents was referred to and they were frequently target group-specific.

- The desire to provide a comprehensive and effective service, coupled with an overlap of target group or agency activities, and sometimes a shortage of current provision, were often reasons for establishing multi-agency working. This was also encouraged by Government support for the notion of 'joined-up' thinking.

- The influence of local authority characteristics was a factor raised by interviewees in a number of different contexts. References were made to the importance of a history of close interagency relationships and multi-agency working, the impact of local Government reorganisation, and the experiences, interests and commitment of staff. These local factors could also be linked to the desire for more multi-agency working, which was cited as a main rationale for the formation of initiatives by 17 per cent of the sample.

The focus or target group

A range of different focuses or target groups for multi-agency initiatives was identified by interviewees. By way of summary:

- The multi-agency initiatives were, in the main, reported by interviewees to be focused on a range of specific target groups: LAC, disaffected pupils, pupils with SEN (including those with speech and language difficulties), pupils with complex needs, children and families with mental health problems, children in need or at risk and early years.

- ◆ A few initiatives, however, had a broader remit, such as those focused on health improvement in schools, strategic planning and those initiatives which sought to provide counselling, advice and mentoring for pupils with problems.

- ◆ Over a fifth of all the initiatives highlighted by interviewees were targeted at LAC, whilst just under a fifth were focused on pupils with SEN (including those with speech and language difficulties), suggesting that these are particular areas of multi-agency interest at this time. Health improvement, strategic planning and disaffected pupils were the next most highly featured areas of multi-agency working identified by interviewees.

The agencies involved

Over half of all the initiatives identified involved all three of the main agencies, i.e. Social Services, Health and Education, whilst just under a third involved Social Services and Education and just under a quarter involved Health and Education. In summary the following points, with regard to the agencies involved, emerged:

- ◆ The agencies involved were often closely associated with the target group or focus of the initiative, Social Services in the case of LAC, for example, and Health in the case of pupils with speech and language difficulties.

- ◆ Initiatives involving all three of the main agencies were commonly found within specific target groups or areas where a three-way interagency response was required because of the complexity of the issues, such as pupils with complex needs and strategic planning.

- ◆ In some particular areas, the lack of Health input was notable, for example, despite the fact that some interviewees recognised a connection between mental health problems and disaffection, involvement of health was lacking in the latter group. This was also notable in initiatives focused on early years.

Within the next phase of the research, the rationale and stimuli for the initiation of multi-agency work with different focuses will be examined in more depth, together with a closer examination of the roles and responsibilities of the different agencies involved. These findings will be presented in the final report.

Finally, within this section of the report, detailed illustrations of initiatives within the different target groups are presented, before we move on to consider the main benefits, challenges and key factors in success associated with the initiatives, as identified by interviewees.

Detailed illustrations of initiatives with different focuses or target groups

Looked-after children

Agencies
Mainly Social Services and Education, with some Health and voluntary sector involvement.

Rationale
Set up in response to local concern about the performance of LAC, this followed a training scheme that had been set up for educational social workers, social workers and child care staff regarding the educational needs of LAC.

Description
A LAC support team which included a senior educational social worker, a senior teacher and a support worker, whose role was to raise the awareness of other professionals regarding LAC, as well as working with children's homes and individual children. The team also developed training schemes for foster carers, child care staff and teachers and addressed policy issues both in schools and with field social workers.

Agencies
Mainly Social Services and Education, but it also involved Health and two voluntary agencies.

Rationale
The LEA was focusing on LAC through Quality Protects. They were successful in being selected by the voluntary agencies involved to receive some money for this initiative.

Description
Senior managers from Social Services and Education developed a prioritised plan for LAC. They identified a variety of aims, including the development of Individual Education Plans for LAC, and working groups were then set up to look at these issues. A senior educational professional with responsibility for LAC was appointed and managed by Social Services. In addition, some staff within Social Services were transferred to the SEN Support Service to enhance the service received by LAC that had been excluded from school.

Speech and language difficulties

Agencies
Mainly Health and Education, with some involvement of Social Services and the voluntary sector.

Rationale
Following an SEN review, there was concern about speech and language issues within the authority, and a headteacher group was set up to examine them. Training for the support assistants was then prioritised on the advice of headteachers.

Description
Teachers and speech and language therapists were employed to develop and deliver a training package to support assistants and teachers in schools. A senior educational psychologist coordinated the programme and a part-time teacher organised it. A full-time teacher worked within the therapy service and a strong partnership with schools had been developed. The LEA was now looking at developing a fully integrated service.

Agencies
Health and Education.

Rationale
The Health Trust was finding it difficult to recruit speech and language therapists and, as a result, waiting lists were long and children with statements were not getting their needs met in mainstream schools. The Health Trust also had a statutory duty to reduce waiting lists.

Description
Speech and language therapists worked in mainstream schools with pupils with identified language difficulties. A programme of training for all school staff was implemented. Within this programme, speech and language therapists worked with small groups of young people alongside teachers and learning support assistants. Alternative models of service delivery and a move away from the off-site clinical model were being examined in order to make provision more effective.

Disaffected pupils

Agencies
Social Services, Health and Education.

Rationale
The LEA previously had an 'out-of-school' panel, but they found that a lot of pupils remained on the list and received limited home tuition because they were often not accessing education for health or social reasons. These cases, therefore, never moved forward and they thought if they could get the other agencies involved they could discuss these cases in detail.

Description
A behaviour management panel composed of 17 people, who included three from Health (a paediatrician, a child and family psychologist and a management representative), a Social Services representative and a range of educational professionals who dealt with pupils out of school. The panel met every six weeks and had a set number of cases to deal with. At strategic level, the group also picked up trends and examined related issues, e.g. Government initiatives.

Agencies
Mainly Social Services and Education, with some Health involvement.

Rationale
A mapping exercise was conducted to find out where the issues and incidences of deprivation were, using indicators such as low educational achievement and disaffection. It was agreed that a multi-agency response was needed to address this because the issue was broader based than just schools. At the same time, a Youth Service review highlighted the need for the service to undertake more outreach work.

Description
Centred on two secondary schools in high areas of deprivation, a multi-agency team was developed to *'encourage a sense of collaboration between young people and adults'*. The team, which included youth workers, EWOs and social workers, worked with pupils on the verge of disaffection or those likely to be excluded from school. A range of strategies was adopted, including one-to-one and group work with pupils, a drop-in service, a parents' support group, a young mothers' group and staff training.

Pupils with complex needs

Agencies
Social Services, Health and Education.

Rationale
When this LEA became a new unitary authority, the need for clarity and transparency of activities, particularly with regard to budgetary responsibilities, was identified. Meetings were held informally, firstly between Social Services and Education, and then including Health, to discuss these issues. The Education and the Social Services' representatives both recognised the need for a multi-agency panel for 'out-of-county' placements and were the main driving force for this initiative.

Description
An 'out-of-authority' placement panel composed of senior officers from each of the three agencies and other principal officers who advised on specific cases. Cases of children with a range of needs, who were therefore difficult to place locally, were examined. The panel discussed issues of agency responsibility and finance for this provision and made decisions about provision for these pupils.

Agencies
Social Services, Health and Education.

Rationale
Initially set up because it was a new authority with a lot of children with complex needs in the area, a joint meeting between the three agencies was held to discuss individual cases where issues had not been resolved and all other strategies had failed. This then progressed to a strategy group as they felt they needed to address issues around the infrastructure, such as funding mechanisms, that supported the professionals working on cases. Work by Young Minds on complex cases in the area and the lack of therapeutic input for children also provided a stimulus for this initiative.

Description
A strategy group with senior management representation that met once every half term. The aims of the group were defined as *'commissioning, providing, shared responsibility, finding solutions, developing systems, looking at resources and identifying shortfalls'*.

Children with mental health problems

Agencies
Health and Education.

Rationale
This initiative was set up because Education staff found it difficult to access mental health services and, where these services did work with children, they tended to focus solely on health objectives. When educational professionals referred children, therefore, they were not meeting educational targets. As they were not able to change the way that the service worked, they decided to enlist their professional support for staff within the Behaviour Support Service. This was also felt to fit closely with mental health intervention at tier two for the Health Advisory Service (HAS) model.

Description
The Behaviour Support Service was supported by the Mental Health Service through consultation with mental heath professionals. A group of staff met with two consultant psychiatrists on Health Authority premises one afternoon each week. They discussed both general issues and specific cases.

Agencies
Social Services, Health and Education.

Rationale
This initiative was set up in response to the HAS Report *Together We Stand*, which empowered the staff within the authority to be able to sell their model of service delivery to council members. The different political culture compared to a few years ago was also influential and this strategy was felt to fit well with what the DfEE and the Department of Health were asking local authorities to do.

Description
The central principle was that mental health is *'everybody's business'*. A Steering Group examined services with regard to the HAS model and conducted a number of pieces of work at different levels. At tier one, this included mental health training for those with direct contact with children, including teachers. At level two, this included three pilot projects challenging behaviour intervention projects with multi-professional teams of primary mental health workers, family support workers, teachers and educational psychologists. At level four, a lot of research on children and young people within specialist provision had been conducted.

Children in need or at risk

Agencies
Social Services and Education (the EWS and the Youth Service) mainly, with involvement of the voluntary sector and the police.

Rationale
Through previous joint working at interagency level, concerns were raised about the vulnerable group of young people involved in prostitution so a discussion forum was set up and information pulled together. It was a recognised local need and all agencies were struggling to meet the needs of these young people so it had the backing of all the agencies. A large interagency meeting was held to discuss the issues and a Steering Group was set up to conduct research into the area. This highlighted that a local project was the best way forward.

Description
A project to which agencies could refer young people found to be involved in prostitution. The project coordinator undertook work in residential settings, worked closely on the street with the police, as well as providing young people with a direct service. Workers also went to schools and provision for excluded pupils to do preventative work and to inform pupils about the service.

Agencies
Social Services, Health and Education.

Rationale
The rationale behind this initiative was to bring all the people for older children in need together into one team to improve coordination between services because a large proportion of them had a multitude of problems and are not dealt with by one agency. Different services were giving conflicting advice to families. A model was developed in which services were flexible and whichever professional families went to for help they were able to provide a holistic assessment and to direct them to the appropriate services.

Description
A discrete group of professionals, including EWOs, social workers and health visitors, that all had a role to play in assessing whether children are in need of additional services over and above what is normally offered, were brought together into a team to do initial assessment and management of cases. Links with other agencies were conducted through specific projects.

21

Early years

Agencies
Mainly Social Services and Education, with some Health involvement.

Rationale
The service was brought together to ensure effective utilisation of local and Government grants in this field. There was already multi-agency work occurring through the Early Years and Child Care Development Partnership drive and the local authority had a statutory responsibility to convene centrally in a multi-agency way. It was reported that 'everyone is now on board'.

Description
Early Years and Child Care Services jointly funded by Education and Social Services, and this had brought together all the developmental, regulatory and provision services into one joint service. A coordinator had the key responsibility for coordinating the partnership and implementing the plan. A broad range of functions was involved, including day care regulation, early education, child care provision, resources and information, etc.

Agencies
Social Services, Health, Education and the voluntary sector.

Rationale
This initiative was set up as a Sure Start initiative through Government funding, but began in a small way and had now been extended considerably. This meant that the service was able to try interventions out in a small way and then broaden them to other deprived areas of the county.

Description
With a target group of parents of children from 0–3 years, the initiative involved a lot of different aspects. This included the provision of a play bus, nursery nurses working in play groups, work in family homes, running a crèche, setting up Book Start and the provision of child minders who also do work on basic skills. The staff was used flexibly and interchangeably and was perceived by parents as a team. The team comprised a coordinator, two nursery nurses from Health, basic skills development workers, tutors, an educational nursery nurse and some volunteer workers.

Strategic planning

Agencies
Mainly Social Services and Education, with some Health involvement.

Rationale
External forces were reported to be the stimulus for this initiative, such as the Government requirement for a 'step change' regarding social inclusion and local political expectations for a structure based on groups of people, rather than separate agency services. An action plan was developed between Education and Social Services and the post described was one outcome from this.

Description
A joint Education and Social Services post to drive and enable joint action between the two agencies and to identify common aims and objectives, to keep a check on performance indicators and to look at initiatives that might benefit both agencies in terms of their targets. This role had included involvement in a number of developments so far, including a joint review of nursery schools and family centres, joint solutions for children out of school and joint training sessions for teachers and carers.

Agencies
Social Services, Health, Education and a range of other agencies, including community partnership, housing and representatives of service users.

Rationale
Whilst this authority had a multi-agency planning group for a long time, it was reported that it had not been working effectively and that the multi-agency aspect was 'being paid lip service to' in that decisions by the group were often overturned by individual agencies. In addition, working groups within agencies had good ideas but there was no structure to support this, so this was reviewed. It was agreed that the group should involve tier two officers and that subgroups would be set up to coordinate efforts across the agencies.

Description
A joint strategic executive in which a large number of agencies were involved and which met monthly to plan strategic developments. There were two main subgroups, children and adults. The children's group involved several different working groups, including those focused on child protection, complex needs, mental health, Quality Protects and early years, as these were seen as main priorities. Each group reported back termly.

Health improvement

Agencies
Social Services, Health and Education

Rationale
It was reported that the Government's Healthy Schools Initiative would provide another way of tackling EDP targets and it was felt that, if schools got their overall ethos right, this would raise standards. Thus, the framework provided by this initiative was felt to suit the authority's needs. In addition, this initiative was influenced by multi-agency work within the EAZ that was reported to have 'made a difference'.

Description
This LEA used the Healthy Schools Initiative as an umbrella for multi-agency working. A Steering Group at officer level and a strategy group met twice a month. The operational group, responsible for delivery, involved tier two and tier three managers. All the agencies were reported to work together to get schools up to the standard required for accreditation. It was run in a pilot group of schools to begin with, in which they were trialling some materials, and Health had seconded a coordinator for this. The initiative built on previous work in the areas of drug education, sex and health education and road safety.

Agencies
The main strategic partnership was between Health and Education, but, at operational level, many agencies were involved, including the police.

Rationale
The World Health Organisation recognised that schools could be valuable settings for health promotion and, in 1993, the authority began a scheme addressing eight areas of school life where health promotion activities were relevant. Then the Government provided money for the development of a national standard. Health in the area was poor, and there was a belief that every opportunity should be taken to improve it.

Description
Schools signed up to the project and were required to set up a team with responsibility for the initiative within their own school, which included teaching and non-teaching staff. The team conducted an audit to identify areas for health improvement, and three key areas for development were identified. With the help of the Healthy Schools Inspector a plan was then implemented and schools themselves assessed to identify if they had met the necessary targets for accreditation.

Counselling, advice and mentoring for young people

Agencies
Health and Education, through the Youth Service.

Rationale
Ten years ago the LEA was approached by the Health Authority to work together to reduce teenage pregnancy. The Health Authority found that young people were not accessing services designed for adults, and the rates of teenage pregnancy had 'gone through the roof', as in other areas of the country. Research showed that youngsters needed a range of services, including advice, information and family planning. A facility was therefore set up in the town centre.

Description
A centre providing advice and information around a range of issues that is a priority for young people. Staffed by a youth worker, nurses and doctors, there was a town centre base at a high-profile site. The centre was open every day and staff from both agencies were always available. Young people were reported to be able to access information and confidential counselling services, and the service had since been extended to isolated outreach areas.

Agencies
Social Services, Education and a voluntary agency.

Rationale
This initiative arose from the local authority's prevention and Family Support Strategy which was developed in 1998. A multi-agency working group was set up to look at family support and this was one of the outcomes. There was also concern about issues for LAC and those on the child protection register and making better use of voluntary agencies.

Description
A counselling and advice service that was also involved in developing surgeries in schools for parents and children. A voluntary agency social worker was based in each school for one day a week. The service was used in different ways in different schools, but the focus was very much on prevention and helping parents deal with problems before they become major.

SEN pupils

Agencies
Social Services, Health, Education, and the voluntary sector.

Rationale
This initiative was a response to a significant increase in the number of autistic children within the area (also mirrored nation-wide) and a problem recognised by all three agencies, thus lending itself to a multi-agency approach. Consultation with all the agencies was reported to be an important part of the development process. Becoming a new unitary authority in 1996 enabled them to make a fresh start and to try out new ideas.

Description
Focused on the needs of autistic children, a specialist autism development worker was appointed through money available within the Health Authority that was set aside for the support of innovative projects. A collaborative bid was put together for the money, which was then used to provide direct case work with children and families, including support in the home, support in schools, training for school staff, as well as to develop a multi-agency approach. The worker was employed by Education although physically they were based within Social Services.

Agencies
Social Services, Health and Education.

Rationale
The Child Development Centre was set up by the Health Authority, and Education had been involved since 1974 because it was thought to be an ideal opportunity to work in a multi-agency way. The social inclusion agenda was reported to have influenced the present remit of the centre as they were now providing more support at the transition into primary school.

Description
Focused on pre-school children with developmental delays who were referred by the health visitor, the centre was operated by the Health Authority, but with input from Social Services and Education. Education staff, for example, provided four teaching groups with the aim of reaching early learning goals. Nursery nurses also had targets for children to achieve linked to early learning goals. Work was undertaken with individuals and with small groups of children. Speech therapists worked alongside teachers with children with language problems. In addition, the social worker provided support for families at home where children had significant social issues or where there was work to be done on parenting. A thorough baseline assessment of children's difficulties was conducted and work undertaken with school staff to develop strategies.

PART 2.
BENEFITS, CHALLENGES AND KEY FACTORS IN SUCCESS

Introduction

During telephone interviews with representatives of 221 different initiatives, interviewees were asked about the benefits, challenges and key factors in success associated with the multi-agency initiatives that they had identified. Their responses to these questions form the focus of this part of the report. Firstly, the benefits of multi-agency working are discussed.

2.1 Benefits

Interviewees were asked what they considered to be the main benefits of multi-agency working to both the target group (in the majority of cases, pupils) and the professionals involved. Firstly, the overall benefits interviewees identified are discussed, followed by the benefits associated with initiatives that involved joint working between the different agencies, i.e. all three agencies, Social Services and Education and Health and Education. Finally, the benefits associated with different focuses or target groups are examined.

2.1.1 The overall benefits identified by interviewees

Table 2.1 shows the overall benefits that were each highlighted by more than ten per cent of interviewees, together with the number and percentage of interviewees who offered them.

The main benefits highlighted were those directly experienced by the professionals involved. Thus, a greater understanding of the roles and responsibilities of different agencies was noted by about a quarter of all interviewees. In particular, some noted that involvement within the initiative had given them a greater understanding of the constraints on other agencies, such that they had more realistic expectations of what they were able to offer. Communication and information sharing between agencies was a key benefit to the professionals involved, noted by about a fifth of the total number of interviewees, with some commenting that the additional information gained was then used to inform their own working practice. The development of effective working relationships between professionals (also noted by about a fifth of interviewees) was also considered a key benefit of the initiatives. Many interviewees highlighted the fact that joint working within the initiative had allowed the agencies to develop their relationship further and, as a result, it was stronger, such that mutual trust had been developed. Interviewees also noted that, as well as raising awareness of the issues linked with the particular work in question within the different agencies, such as the needs of LAC, working together within the initiatives also provided professionals with an opportunity to discuss, and therefore resolve, issues that had previously created barriers between them and had inhibited multi-agency working. Improved collaboration, shared knowledge, skills and expertise, as well as joint ownership of the issues were also highlighted by over a tenth of all interviewees. Illustrations for each of the benefits raised by interviewees are provided on the following pages.

Table 2.1 The benefits identified by interviewees from over ten per cent of the total sample of 221 initiatives, in rank order

Benefit	Number	Percentage (N=221)
Understanding roles and responsibilities	53	24
Support for inclusion	50	23
Information sharing or communication	47	21
Raised awareness	43	19
Improved working relationships	40	18
Impact on other joint work	40	18
Opportunity to discuss or resolve issues	40	18
Improved collaboration	38	17
Shared knowledge, skills or expertise	35	16
Joint ownership	33	15
Direct benefits to pupils (mainly raised attainment)	33	15
Improved access to funding or resources	33	15
Direct benefits to schools or teachers (mainly support)	32	14
Holistic approach	31	14
Needs addressed more appropriately	29	13
Coordinated approach	27	12
Cost-effective or efficient	25	11

Interviewees were able to give more than one response, and therefore percentages do not sum to 100 per cent.
Source: Telephone interviews in Phase One of the NFER study, 2000.

With regard to the benefits to the target group that were raised, indirect benefits, such as a holistic approach, a coordinated approach and one which met the needs of the target group more effectively, were each raised by over one-tenth of all the interviewees. Other indirect benefits to pupils of note, although raised by less than ten per cent of interviewees, included access to alternative strategies, early intervention, the ability to identify gaps in provision, having one point of access for the different agencies, a quicker and more immediate response to problems, and a consistent approach across the agencies. Direct benefits to pupils, on the other hand, perhaps because of the nature of the initiatives or the emphasis on the 'multi-agency' benefits, were not raised as often, with the most frequent one (highlighted by 13 interviewees) being raised achievement and the next most frequent one the individual support provided for pupils. Support for schools or teachers, on the other hand, was raised by about a tenth of interviewees, whilst support for parents was also noted by only 11 interviewees and therefore is not shown in the table.

Illustrations of the main benefits identified by interviewees

Understanding roles and responsibilities	Within one initiative, targeted at disaffected pupils, professionals within Social Services were reported to understand '*the systemic elements in schools*' and '*the demands on schools and teachers*' better. Another interviewee, involved in an initiative focused on health improvement, reported that Health professionals were now '*valuing how youth workers can engage with young people*' and that youth workers now understood '*the structures and roles within the Health Service.*'
Support for inclusion	Having a forum for dealing with pupils with complex needs was reported by one interviewee to '*force agencies* [Social Services, Health and Education] *to look at solutions within the area*' and therefore to maintain children in local provision. Within an initiative targeting LAC, one school, it was reported, had assigned a senior member of staff to work with Social Services' staff in an attempt to reduce the number of LAC excluded from school. By addressing difficulties early within an initiative focused on children in need, one of the main benefits was that a smaller proportion of children were reported to enter formal schooling with difficulties and they were cited as being '*more receptive to formal schooling*'.
Information sharing or communication	A monthly update of the LAC within the area from Social Services was considered beneficial as this gave Education staff '*a means of planning ... and looking at services and resources available*'. Similarly, within an SEN panel meeting, Education was cited as providing valuable information because it was felt that Social Services professionals would not know '*whether it is a good or bad educational placement*'.
Raised awareness	One interviewee stated that a LAC initiative, involving all three agencies, had made schools '*more sensitive to the needs and circumstances of LAC*', whilst an SEN initiative involving Health and Education was reported to have '*raised the profile of autism*' and '*increased its acceptance as a profound and debilitating condition*' amongst professionals. Involvement in a 'counselling' initiative, a joint venture between Health and Education, was felt to have influenced the relationship health workers had with young people so that they '*understand what is going on for them*' and '*why they behave in a particular way*'.
Improved working relationships	One interviewee stated that one of the main benefits of a strategic planning group involving all three agencies was '*personal and professional respect*', such that, when concerns were raised, they were '*treated seriously and urgently*', whilst another reported that close working relationships with Health senior managers in a similar forum had led to '*a feeling of confidence and mutual trust*'. An educational professional involved in a mental health initiative involving all three agencies stated that, in terms of benefits, '*all barriers*' and '*suspicions and territory squabbles*' were beginning to disappear.

Impact on other joint work	One interviewee involved in an initiative focused on children with mental health problems involving all three agencies stated that all projects were '*part of the global whole*' and that there were '*links with other work*'. The instigation of other joint work was a particularly beneficial outcome of strategic planning groups involving all three agencies, and one interviewee stated that '*numerous tangible outcomes*' had been developed and '*come to fruition*' as a result of the group driving them forward.
Opportunity to discuss or resolve issues	One interviewee reported that the professionals involved in a strategic planning group, from all three agencies, were '*no longer like colleagues in different statutory organisations*' and that they could '*sit down and discuss things without going through the red tape*'. Another interviewee stated that involvement in a 'speech and language' initiative meant that Health and Educational professionals regularly talked together and, whilst it had not eliminated issues about different cultures and different practices, it had '*provided a forum in which we can address them*'.
Improved collaboration	Within a strategic planning forum, involving a range of agencies, the educational personnel reported that they had developed closest links with the police and that, when there is an issue about risk management, there is now '*an immediate and collaborative response*'.
Shared knowledge, skills or expertise	From a manager perspective, within an 'early years' initiative involving all three agencies, the greatest benefit was felt to be '*the skill sharing and the knowledge sharing*' between professionals, and there was reported to be '*a lot of cross-fertilisation and collaboration going on*'.
Joint ownership	One interviewee reported that involvement in an initiative focused on LAC, a joint venture between Education and Social Services, had '*changed the culture*' and that there was now '*a corporate responsibility for the problem*'. They stated that, if LAC were not in school, for example, '*all the agencies have to look at solving the problem*'.
Direct benefits to pupils	In addition to raised attainment, particularly with regard to LAC, greater continuity for young people was cited as a benefit within an initiative targeted at disaffected pupils involving all three agencies as '*their day can be so fragmented*' and '*the school day not joined up to the rest of their lives*'. '*A one-stop shop*' approach adopted within a 'counselling' initiative between Health and Education was considered by one interviewee as beneficial for young people because they did not have to '*move from pillar to post – it is all under one roof*'.
Improved access to funding or resources	Having a strategic planning group involving all three agencies was reported by one interviewee to provide '*a plethora of opportunities*' concerning the social inclusion agenda as it meant that joint bids for funding were facilitated.
Benefits to schools or teachers	One interviewee highlighted the direct benefits to schools of a Health and Education joint initiative focused on pupils with speech and language difficulties as assistants and teachers within schools were trained to understand speech and language problems.
Holistic approach	A joint Education and Social Services initiative targeting pupils with complex needs was felt by one interviewee to enable the professionals involved to '*see their educational needs in the context of their overall social situation*'. An interviewee involved in an initiative focused on health improvement involving Health and Education stated that joint working had enabled them to '*see a broader framework*' and s/he reported that, whilst before they might focus on '*teenage pregnancy*', they were now focused more on '*mental health issues, such as self-esteem and looking at where things like behaviour fit in*'.
Needs met more appropriately	Having the different perspectives of Education and Social Services for disaffected pupils was felt by one interviewee to provide '*a holistic view of needs*', to ensure appropriate provision and to facilitate '*the best match*', whilst having a joint assessment between the three agencies for SEN pupils meant for one interviewee that they could '*respond more flexibly to the child's needs*'.

Coordinated approach	The main benefit, reported by an interviewee involved in an 'early years' initiative involving all three agencies, was that the public only have to go to one service and they were '*all singing from the same song sheet*'.
Cost-effective or efficient	A '*mapping exercise*' conducted between the three agencies as part of a strategic planning group was reported to reveal a lot of duplication and hence to enable resources to be targeted more effectively.

Source: Telephone interviews in Phase One of the NFER study, 2000.

Benefits classified as 'strategic-level' were also highlighted. Support for the process of inclusion, for example, was also raised as a key benefit of these multi-agency initiatives by almost a quarter of all interviewees, although they expressed this in different ways. Joint working was considered in some cases to support inclusion by reducing the exclusion of pupils and improving their attendance, or by maintaining and reintegrating pupils into mainstream schools and, in other cases, by preventing the need for specialist provision or out-of-county placement, thus maintaining pupils in local provision. Other more strategic-level benefits raised frequently by interviewees included the knock-on effect that joint working within one initiative had for other areas of work (noted by almost a fifth of all interviewees). Multi-agency working within one initiative, for example, was reported to have led to joint working in other areas because of the working relationships that had been established. Improved access to funding and resources at strategic level (noted by over one-sixth) was also considered a benefit. Interviewees highlighted, for example, that joint working enabled them to bid for funding which they might otherwise not be able to access because multi-agency involvement was a requirement for the bid. Other strategic benefits of interest also raised, although by less than ten per cent of interviewees, included better planning, the development of new models of working or new services, the avoidance of duplication, creative or radical thinking and having a clearer focus for the work.

2.1.2 Benefits associated with work between different agencies

Table 2.2 shows the main benefits interviewees identified in connection with initiatives involving different agencies, each in rank order.

Some benefits featured in joint working in all three groups, i.e. these appeared to be benefits gained regardless of which agencies were involved. These included understanding the roles and responsibilities of other agencies, joint ownership of the issues and the needs of the target group, impact on other areas of joint working and adopting a holistic approach to problems. In contrast, some benefits, such as improved access to funding and resources (mainly through joint funding arrangements), cost-effectiveness and the ability to provide a seamless service or identify gaps in provision, were considered to be a benefit only where all three agencies were involved. Other benefits appeared to be a feature only where Social Services and Education were involved, such as raised awareness (the most frequently mentioned benefit in this group). Similarly, some benefits only featured

Table 2.2   The benefits interviewees identified in connection with initiatives involving different agencies, each presented in rank order

Social Services, Health and Education	Social Services and Education	Health and Education
• Information sharing or communication	• Raised awareness	• Support for schools
• Improved access to funding or resources	• Understanding roles and responsibilities	• Enhancing the skills of teachers
• Improved working relationships	• Support for inclusion	• Impact on other joint work
• Needs addressed more appropriately	• Information sharing or communication	• Access to specialist input
• Understanding roles and responsibilities	• Holistic approach	• Improved collaboration
• Opportunity to discuss/address issues	• Needs addressed more appropriately	• Shared knowledge, skills or expertise
• Impact on other joint work	• Improved collaboration	• Understanding roles and responsibilities
• Holistic approach	• Joint ownership	• Improved working relationships
• Seamless provision or gaps identified	• Coordinated approach	• Support for inclusion
• Cost-effective or efficient	• Opportunity to discuss or resolve issues	• Joint ownership
• Joint ownership	• Impact on other joint work	• Holistic approach

Source: Telephone interviews in Phase One of the NFER study, 2000.

where Health and Education were involved, such as support for schools, enhancing the skills of teachers, access to specialist input and shared knowledge, and expertise, which all featured highly. Support for inclusion, on the other hand, appeared to be a benefit accrued through joint working between Social Services and Education and Health and Education, rather than through work amongst all the three agencies. This may reflect the more operational focus of these initiatives, compared to the strategic focus where all three agencies were involved. In addition, some benefits, such as pupils' needs being addressed more appropriately and the opportunity to discuss and address issues, were notably absent from joint working between Health and Education.

2.1.3 Benefits associated with different focuses/target groups

The main benefits identified by interviewees in association with initiatives with different target groups are shown in Table 2.3. From this data the following points emerged:

- Where initiatives tended to involve a decision-making forum, such as in addressing the needs of pupils with complex needs and strategic planning, interviewees highlighted more strategic-level benefits, such as cost-effectiveness, shared funding, the opportunity to discuss and resolve issues, better planning and, commonly, the ability to identify gaps in provision.

- The most common benefits interviewees raised were often specific to the target group. Thus, the main benefit identified in the case of work around LAC was the raised awareness of their educational and social needs amongst professionals, and, in the case of disaffected pupils, the way in which multi-agency work supported the process of inclusion was a key benefit.

- In addition, where children were specifically targeted, the fact that their needs were able to be addressed more appropriately through joint working was often raised, as for children with mental health problems, disaffected pupils and those with speech and language difficulties.

- Understanding the roles and responsibilities of other professionals was also a common feature in many groups, but was particularly noted by a number of interviewees in association with work centred on LAC, SEN pupils, children with mental health problems and children in need or at risk. This might indicate a need to raise professional awareness of the role of different agencies within these areas through multi-agency work of this nature.

- The benefits interviewees associated with SEN pupils were notable in that a number focused on benefits to parents, as well as those to professionals, such as having one point of access to all the agencies and support for parents.

- In contrast, benefits identified by interviewees in the areas of health improvement and speech and language difficulties focused on the additional support and expertise that was offered to schools, and those associated with counselling, advice and mentoring focused on support for young people and addressing their needs.

- Multi-agency work focused on children in need or at risk was felt to provide a flexibility of approach otherwise not available and, in addition to benefits to professionals, a holistic approach and a quick or more immediate response to children's needs.

- Multi-agency work in early years has been a requirement for a considerable time and has been long established and, perhaps because of this, the main benefit highlighted in connection with this work was its impact on other areas of joint work. Interviewees often noted that a single piece of joint working of this nature, if successful, often led to further interagency work in other fields.

Table 2.3   The main benefits associated with different target groups

Looked-after children
- raised awareness
- understanding roles and responsibilities
- information sharing or communication
- improved educational achievement

SEN pupils
- understanding roles and responsibilities
- one point of access for pupils and parents
- information sharing or communication
- support for parents

Pupils with speech and language difficulties
- enhancing skills of school staff
- new models or new ways of working
- specialist input for schools
- needs addressed more appropriately
- support for inclusion

Disaffected pupils
- support for inclusion
- needs addressed more appropriately
- shared knowledge, skills and expertise
- holistic approach
- understanding roles and responsibilities
- early intervention
- information sharing or communication

Pupils with complex needs
- cost-effective or efficient
- support for inclusion
- joint ownership
- improved access to funding or resources
- seamless provision or gaps identified

Children with mental health problems
- understanding roles and responsibilities
- new models or new ways of working
- needs addressed more appropriately
- opportunity to discuss or resolve issues

Children in need or at risk
- flexibility
- understanding roles and responsibilities
- improved collaboration
- shared knowledge, skills and expertise
- joint ownership
- holistic approach
- quick or immediate response
- opportunity to discuss or resolve issues

Early years
- impact on other joint work
- improved collaboration
- improved educational achievement
- improved working relationships
- information sharing or communication
- seamless provision or gaps identified
- coherent provision

Counselling, advice and mentoring for pupils
- focus on young people
- seamless provision or gaps identified
- support for young people
- opportunity to discuss or resolve issues
- improved access to funding or resources
- understanding roles and responsibilities

Health improvement
- support for schools
- links with other work
- improved collaboration
- improved access to funding or resources
- understanding roles and responsibilities
- improved working relationships
- holistic approach

Strategic planning
- opportunity to discuss or resolve issues
- information sharing or communication
- impact on other joint work
- understanding roles and responsibilities
- improved working relationships
- better planning
- common aims

Source: Telephone interviews in Phase One of the NFER study, 2000.

2.2 Challenges

Interviewees were asked to identify the challenges associated with multi-agency working within the initiatives. The first section covers the overall challenges identified by interviewees, the next moves on to look at the challenges associated with particular initiatives and the agencies involved, and the final section discusses the challenges associated with the different target groups involved.

2.2.1 The overall challenges identified

Table 2.4 shows the main challenges that interviewees highlighted, together with the numbers and percentages of interviewees nominating them.

Table 2.4   The challenges identified by interviewees from over five per cent of the total sample of 221 initiatives, in rank order

Challenge	Number	Percentage (N=221)
Funding or resources	70	32
Time	30	14
Different priorities or agendas	22	10
Getting others on board	19	9
Different structures or systems	18	8
Different approaches or ways of working	18	8
Information sharing	17	8
Different cultures or perspectives	17	8
Clarifying issues or definitions	15	7
Involving Health	14	6
Overcoming professional boundaries	14	6
Personnel changes	13	6
Government legislation or initiatives	13	6
Initial setting-up period	12	5
Overcoming professional mistrust	12	5
Adapting to or accepting change	11	5
Ensuring commitment	11	5
Management and supervision	11	5

Interviewees were able to give more than one response, and therefore percentages do not sum to 100 per cent.
Source: Telephone interviews in Phase One of the NFER study, 2000.

Almost a third (32 per cent) of interviewees highlighted funding and resource issues as the main challenge facing them in implementing multi-agency initiatives. In many cases, the funding was finite, and ensuring sustainability once it ceased was considered to be a major concern. Difficulties in ensuring equity of funding from all partner agencies were also raised as an issue, as there was often felt to be an element of protectiveness about budgets. 'Joined-up' budgets were felt to be one way to alleviate this problem. The next most frequently identified challenge, although only highlighted by just over one in ten (14 per cent) interviewees, was time. The time commitment needed to set up initiatives was mentioned, as was the subsequent amount of time needed for the work involved, for meetings and administration, often alongside a whole range of other commitments. Also referred to was the time involved in developing relationships with other agencies. Although difficult to find, this was believed to be a worthwhile investment, as it would produce time savings and improve working practices in the future. One in ten interviewees referred to different agency priorities or agendas as a potential for misunderstanding. It was thought to be important to engage all partners equally in all the issues, not just the ones that affected their agency, a factor that concomitantly impacted on the distribution of resources.

A range of other challenges was then highlighted by slightly less than one in ten interviewees. Getting others on board, for example schools, parents or community groups, was the most frequently raised of these. It was felt to be difficult at times to convince others that they had a part to play in an initiative. Schools had to be convinced to commit teacher time and scarce resources, whilst for parents, change often produced anxiety and they had to be persuaded that a particular initiative was the appropriate approach to take. At the same time, there was sometimes an element of persuading others who had been working in the area for a long time that there might be a better way of doing it. Differences between agencies were often a challenge, in particular different structures which sometimes worked against each other, different approaches or ways of working which required negotiation to identify the most appropriate way forward, and different cultures or perspectives which necessitated discussion to establish a common ground. Information sharing was sometimes problematic, especially where IT systems differed: making these compatible then represented a significant investment in the technology. Each agency was involved in collecting data for its own purposes which did not always mesh with each other. One way forward was felt to be a common information collection and monitoring system. Examples of some of the comments made by interviewees are shown in the chart above.

Just over one in 20 interviewees referred to challenges such as the need to clarify issues or definitions, the difficulties inherent in involving Health as a partner agency, overcoming professional boundaries ('preciousness'), personnel changes and Government legislation or initiatives which impacted on the work of the initiative. One in 20 highlighted difficulties, often logistical, in the initial setting-up period, the challenge of overcoming professional mistrust, adapting to, or accepting, change, ensuring the commitment of those involved, and management and supervision issues.

Examples of the main challenges identified by interviewees

Funding or resources	In addition to concerns about adequate funding, joint funding and resources were noted by interviewees to be a particular challenge. Within an Education and Social Services initiative focused on LAC, for example, the money was reported to come from '*two separate camps*' and there was felt to be '*a lot of defensiveness about which is my bit and which is your bit*'. Another interviewee, involved in a joint initiative between Education and Social Services targeted at LAC, stated that, whilst '*the Government talks about joined-up thinking and working*', joined-up funding was what was needed. Lack of this was felt to make joint working very difficult '*because people get defensive about their own department*'.
Time	Whilst it was recognised by some interviewees that joint working between all three agencies gave '*a better outcome*', '*time savings*' or '*better working practice in the future*', it was also reported to take time to set up and that '*it 'absorbs resources in the process*'.
Different priorities or agendas	Within an Education and Health initiative focused on pupils with speech and language difficulties, one interviewee reported that '*people come from different places*' and '*the education agenda might be about attainment, whilst the language therapy agenda might be that children understand language and can communicate better*'. An interviewee involved in a joint Education and Social Services initiative focused on children with learning difficulties felt that, without good informal working relationships beforehand, there was '*great potential for misunderstanding when approaches and agendas can be so different*'. Professionals from both Education and Social Services working with LAC were reported by one interviewee to have to '*change the way they work*' as they were still felt to '*see their own issues as a priority*'.
Getting others on board	Involving parents of children with speech and language difficulties and persuading them that joint working between Education and Health was '*the right approach and a better service*', as well as involving the voluntary sector in planning, were reported to be key challenges within one initiative. In another initiative, where Social Services and Education worked together, it was reported to be difficult to persuade people who have been doing a job a long time that there may be a better way of doing it with another agency.
Different structures/ systems	Different legal frameworks within Education and Social Services meant that, according to one interviewee, '*you can get stuck on definitions*'.
Different approaches or ways of working	One interviewee, involved in an SEN initiative involving all three agencies, reported that there were often '*different opinions about the way forward*' and that this was especially the case where young children were concerned.
Different cultures or perspectives	'*Inevitable cultural differences between* [Education and Social Services] *departments*', noted by one interviewee involved with LAC, '*had to be worked through to build confidence and understanding.*' S/he stated that it was easy, for example, for Education to '*wax lyrical about SATs results*' and for Social Services to '*wax lyrical about care plans*'.
Information sharing	Referring to all three agencies and their involvement with SEN pupils, one interviewee stated that '*each has a different system and we have been told there are means of marrying them up, but we may have to make a significant investment in IT or it won't have the potential we want it to*'. Similarly, with regard to Education and Social Services involvement with LAC, another interviewee stated that '*each department collects its own data for its own purposes and they would not easily mesh with each other*'.

Source: Telephone interviews in Phase One of the NFER study, 2000.

2.2.2 Challenges associated with work between different agencies

Table 2.5 shows, in rank order, the main challenges identified by interviewees according to the different agencies involved in the initiatives.

Some challenges were identified that impacted on joint working regardless of which agencies were involved, most notably funding and resources, but also including time and different approaches or ways of working. Some challenges were felt to affect joint working most when all three agencies were involved, for example the need to clarify issues and/or definitions, overcoming professional boundaries, the effect of Government legislation or initiatives, and personnel changes. This perhaps reflects the difficulty of involving a number of professionals from different agencies with so many contradictory influences. Challenges raised for initiatives where only Social Services and Education were involved included the problem of different timescales and planning cycles and involving Health, when the latter had perhaps not traditionally been involved to the same extent in multi-agency activity. Challenges highlighted within initiatives involving only Health and Education included clarifying roles and responsibilities, competing priorities or demands, recruitment issues, and demand.

Different structures or systems, different priorities or agendas and information sharing were identified as challenges in initiatives where all three agencies were involved, as well as where only Social Services and Education were involved, but not where only Health and Education were involved. The challenge to get others on board and differences in cultures or perspectives were highlighted in joint working involving Social Services and Education, and in joint working involving Health and Education, but not where all three agencies were involved.

Table 2.5   The challenges interviewees identified in connection with initiatives involving different agencies, in rank order

Social Services, Health and Education	Social Services and Education	Health and Education
• Funding or resources	• Funding or resources	• Funding or resources
• Different priorities or agendas	• Information sharing	• Time
• Time	• Getting others on board	• Different cultures or perspectives
• Different structures or systems	• Time	• Clarifying roles or responsibilities
• Clarifying issues or definitions	• Different approaches or ways of working	• Different approaches or ways of working
• Overcoming professional boundaries	• Different structures or systems	• Getting others on board
• Information sharing	• Involving Health	• Competing priorities or demands
• Government legislation or initiatives	• Different cultures or perspectives	• Recruitment
• Different approaches or ways of working	• Different priorities or agendas	• Demand
• Personnel changes	• Different timescales or cycles	

Source: Telephone interviews in Phase One of the NFER study, 2000.

2.2.3 Challenges associated with different focuses/target groups

Table 2.6 shows the main challenges identified by interviewees according to the focus or target group of the particular initiative. Points of interest to emerge from this chart included:

- Funding or resource issues were highlighted as challenges for initiatives involving all target groups except those involving work with disaffected pupils and with children in need or at risk. Challenges for both of these initiatives were most notably time, but also getting others on board, particularly schools in the case of disaffected pupils. This perhaps reflects the current pressures on schools in terms of league tables and the requirement to meet Government targets.

- Challenges for initiatives with a focus on LAC included information collection and sharing, and overcoming professional barriers or protectiveness.

- Challenges for initiatives focused on speech and language difficulties, as well as the funding issues already referred to, included difficulties in recruiting experienced speech and language therapists and the time to develop a new way of working.

- Interestingly, a challenge identified for multi-agency work with an early years focus was professional readjustment. There was believed to be a need for agencies to take the work more seriously, perhaps echoed in the difficulty highlighted by some interviewees of involving Health in the work.

- Apart from funding, challenges associated with work with pupils with complex needs focused notably on the very complexity of the issues involved, which sometimes could be exacerbated by different agency regulations and legal requirements. At the same time, schools and parents often had very different agendas.

- Problems of sharing information and differences between agencies in, for example, priorities or agendas, structures, the effects of Government legislation and in their understanding of the issues involved, were identified as challenges for initiatives with a focus on strategic planning.

- Differences in approaches, agendas and definitions were also identified as challenges for initiatives with a counselling, advice and mentoring focus. At the same time, interviewees commented on staff shortages, the difficulty of addressing young people's mental health needs within the work, and on the challenge presented by the new Children's Services Plan in terms of strategic planning.

Table 2.6 The main challenges associated with different target groups

Looked-after children	SEN pupils	Pupils with speech and language difficulties
• funding or resources • information collection and sharing • getting others to take responsibility or do their bit • professional barriers or protectiveness • getting others on board • recruiting and keeping the right staff	• funding or resources • commitment and getting all on board • time due to other priorities	• time due to other priorities • recruiting experienced speech and language therapists • funding or resources • time to develop a new way of working

Disaffected pupils	Pupils with complex needs	Children with mental health problems
• time for the groundwork • confidentiality • getting schools on board	• funding or resources • complexity of the issues • different agency regulations and legal requirements • different agendas of schools and parents	• funding or resources • different priorities or agendas • management • proving effectiveness • different structures • staff shortages and recruitment • competing priorities

Children in need or at risk	Early years	Counselling, advice and mentoring for pupils
• time • commitment or getting people on board • clarifying roles and responsibilities • different approaches or ways of working • administration	• funding or resources • coordination • professional readjustment • involving Health	• staff shortages and turnover • different approaches • different priorities or agendas • funding • clarifying definitions • addressing young people's mental health needs • new Children's Services Plan guidance

Health improvement	Strategic planning	
• time • funding or resources • clarifying roles and responsibilities • staff changes • getting schools on board • different cultures or perspectives	• funding or resources • information sharing • different priorities or agendas • different structures • time • Government legislation or initiatives • clarifying issues or definitions	

Source: Telephone interviews in Phase One of the NFER study, 2000.

2.3 Key factors in success

Interviewees were asked to identify the key factors that made the initiative they had highlighted a success, particularly in view of the fact that it was a piece of joint working. Firstly, the overall key factors are discussed; then those associated with the work of different agencies and the different target groups are examined.

2.3.1 The overall key factors

Table 2.7 shows the main key factors that interviewees highlighted, together with the number of interviewees nominating them and their percentage of the total sample.

Overwhelmingly, commitment to, or willingness to be involved in, multi-agency work was identified as the main key factor, nominated by over 40 per cent of interviewees. The second highest factor, raised by about a quarter of all interviewees, was the need for good working relationships. Having someone to lead or drive the initiative forward and a clear focus for the work were also nominated by about a fifth of interviewees, whilst the need to establish common aims or shared agendas and to have adequate joint funding and resources also featured highly. It was also felt important to involve the relevant people and for those who were involved to recognise the need for multi-agency input and the benefits that were gained from joint working, as well as for aims and roles to be clear to all those involved. Joint ownership, communication and information sharing, the development of trust (which interviewees often said took time) and understanding each other's roles and responsibilities were also considered key factors, each nominated by about a tenth of all interviewees.

Table 2.7   The key factors in the success of initiatives each nominated by interviewees from over ten per cent of the total sample of 221 initiatives, in rank order

Key factor	Number	Percentage (N=221)
Commitment or willingness	93	42
Good working relationships	53	24
Leadership or drive	41	19
Focus	39	18
Common aims	36	16
Funding or resources	36	16
Involving relevant people	29	13
Recognised need	29	13
Clarity	26	12
Joint ownership	23	10
Information sharing or communication	22	10
Trust	21	10
Understanding roles and responsibilities	19	9

Interviewees were able to give more than one response, and therefore percentages do not sum to 100 per cent.
Source: Telephone interviews in Phase One of the NFER study, 2000.

Illustrations of the main key factors identified by interviewees are given below.

Illustrations of the main key factors identified by interviewees

Commitment or willingness	**Commitment or willingness** The importance of having the commitment to an Education/Health initiative targeted at pupils with SEN, for the professionals involved to give sufficient time and for them to deal effectively with any issues that arose '*so that people are not tempted to take their bat home*' was raised by one interviewee. Similarly, the importance of keeping talking '*even when it was getting painful*' was raised by an interviewee involved in an initiative focused on LAC, whilst the need for staff to '*believe that it is important*' was raised by another involved in early years, both joint ventures between all three agencies.
Good working relationships	One interviewee, involved in an early years partnership between Education and Social Services, stated that '*it comes down to relationships*', and s/he stressed the need to get on with each other and '*stop fighting your own corners*'. '*Professional trust and honesty*' and being '*challenging but respectful*' were referred to as key factors by an interviewee involved in an initiative focused on pupils with complex needs involving all three of the main agencies
Leadership or drive	Interviewees referred to '*having somebody that pushes*', someone who '*will not let the issue go*' and '*a person who champions the cause and follows it through*' in connection with LAC and joint working between Education and Social Services. Another interviewee, again referring to joint working between Education and Social Services, but focused on early years, stated that '*You have to have support from the top if you want to survive, develop and make a difference*'.
Focus	The fact that one initiative, targeted at pupils with complex needs and involving all three agencies, had '*grown from the needs of the local community*' and '*satisfied a clear need*' was felt to be a key factor in its success for one interviewee. Where Education and Social Services were '*focused on the end-product*' the situation for LAC was reported to have been '*enhanced*' and it had been made easier for each of the agencies '*to value each other's contributions*'.
Common aims	Within an 'early years' initiative involving all three agencies, one interviewee reported that you have to '*put your personal or professional agenda aside, on a back burner*' in order to get a common aim or vision. Another interviewee recognised that, where children with mental health problems were concerned, all three of the main agencies had different priorities and the key factor was '*how you can match them to find a solution to help each other address them*'.
Funding or resources	Where there had been '*no demarcation of funding, no quibbling about funding issues and a shared budget*' between the three agencies, this was felt to have been a key factor in the success of an initiative aimed at pupils with complex needs. As well as joint funding, it was also felt important that funding and resources were established long term (for more than three years), as this was considered essential '*to get* [joint working between the three agencies] *off the ground properly*' and '*to ensure sustainability*', as noted by an interviewee within an initiative focused on LAC.
Involving relevant people	A critical factor within an initiative targeted at pupils with complex needs was felt to have been the involvement of the Health provider and purchaser in meetings between the three agencies because '*unless you have the purse holder you cannot do anything*'.
Recognised need	'*Acceptance*' by the three departments of the need '*to find joint solutions*' with regard to pupils with complex needs was highlighted by one interviewee, whilst others noted the importance of staff being able to see the benefits of joint working.
Clarity	Clarity was considered a key factor by an interviewee involved in a LAC initiative involving all three agencies, who noted that '*otherwise there is a danger that nothing gets done*'.
Joint ownership	Within another initiative focused on LAC, the key factor was reported to have been '*understanding and accepting corporate responsibility*', whilst '*making joint decisions*' was felt to be a critical factor in an SEN initiative, both involving all three agencies.

Source: Telephone interviews in Phase One of the NFER study, 2000.

2.3.2 Key factors associated with the work of different agencies

Table 2.8 shows the key factors associated with work between the different agencies, and it can be seen that commitment and a willingness to be involved in multi-agency work and good relationships between the professionals involved were overwhelmingly key factors in all multi-agency working regardless of the agencies involved. The need for someone to lead the work and drive it forward also appeared to be a high priority for interviewees regardless of the agencies concerned, although particularly relevant where all three agencies were involved. In addition, joint funding and resources were a key factor within all multi-agency work, but again particularly important where all three agencies were concerned.

In work between Social Services and Education the need to have a clear focus was raised by many interviewees, indicating perhaps a concern that work between these two agencies might easily stray into other, less relevant areas. In addition, sharing joint responsibility was also considered especially important where Social Services and Education were involved. In contrast, identification of common aims between the agencies and the need to make sure that the relevant professionals were involved was felt to be particularly important where all three agencies and where Health and Education were involved. This was felt to be critical where the right people were needed for decisions to be made. Some interviewees, for example, referred to the division within Health of purchaser and provider sections and the need often to have both represented where relevant. On the other hand, in both work between Social Services and Education and Health and Education, it was felt important for the professionals involved to recognise the need for joint working and to be able to identify the benefits.

Other key factors for work between Social Services and Education (although not raised by sufficient interviewees to be shown in the table) included the requirement for professionals to be non-territorial and to be given training and support, as well as having the backing of managers at strategic level, and the need for multi-agency work to be closely linked to the Government's agenda. Other key factors noted by interviewees in connection with work between Health and Education, in contrast, included professional meetings and quality staff. Interviewees particularly highlighted the need for staff with credibility within both agencies, who, they pointed out, were often those with a background of working within both agencies.

Table 2.8   The key factors in success interviewees identified in connection with initiatives involving different agencies, each in rank order

Social Services, Health and Education	Social Services and Education	Health and Education
• commitment or willingness	• commitment or willingness	• commitment or willingness
• good working relationships	• focus	• good working relationships
• leadership or drive	• good working relationships	• involving relevant people
• common aims	• leadership or drive	• common aims
• funding or resources	• responsibility	• leadership or drive
• focus	• recognised need	• funding or resources
• involving relevant people	• funding or resources	• recognised need
• clarity	• common aims	• focus
• information sharing or communication	• information sharing or communication	• time
• trust	• understanding roles and responsibilities	• clarity

Source: Telephone interviews in Phase One of the NFER study, 2000.

2.3.3 Key factors associated with different target groups or focuses

Table 2.9 shows the key factors associated with different target groups. It is notable again that commitment and good working relationships were key factors regardless of the target group or focus for the work. Involvement of the relevant people also featured highly in initiatives within a number of the different target groups, such as pupils with complex needs and in strategic planning, as did also funding and resources, as in work targeted at SEN pupils and LAC.

. On the other hand, the need for regular and professional meetings was particularly highlighted where strategic planning was involved, whilst the importance of groundwork and laying the foundations for multi-agency work was felt by interviewees to be particularly relevant in work centred on pupils with speech and language difficulties. Trust was highlighted as a particular key factor in initiatives focused on pupils with complex needs and counselling, advice and mentoring, whilst time and the ability to discuss and resolve issues were also considered important where pupils with complex needs were concerned. This might reflect the difficult nature of decisions having to be made for these pupils and the fact that joint funding and large sums of money were often involved. Where SEN pupils, LAC and disaffected pupils were concerned, interviewees highlighted that it was important that there was a clear focus on the needs of these vulnerable young people within multi-agency work.

Table 2.9   The main key factors associated with different target groups

Looked-after children	SEN pupils	Pupils with speech and language difficulties
• commitment or willingness • funding or resources • good working relationships • joint ownership • focus • clarity • common aims	• commitment or willingness • focus • good working relationships • funding or resources • common aims • leadership or drive • sharing information and communication	• common aims • commitment or willingness • involving relevant people • groundwork • funding or resources
Disaffected pupils	**Pupils with complex needs**	**Children with mental health problems**
• commitment or willingness • focus • information sharing or communication • involving relevant people • valuing others' contributions	• good working relationships • recognised need • commitment or willingness • involving relevant people • trust • time • discuss or resolve issues	• commitment or willingness • clarity • joint ownership • good working relationships
Children in need or at risk	**Early years**	**Counselling, advice and mentoring for pupils**
• commitment or willingness • recognised need • good working relationships • common aims	• commitment or willingness • good working relationships • funding or resources • involving relevant people • quality of staff • focus	• trust • independent facilitator • young people involved
Health improvement	**Strategic planning**	
• commitment or willingness • involving relevant people • linked to Government strategy • leadership or drive • common aims • good working relationships	• commitment or willingness • regular or professional meetings • good working relationships • common aims • involving relevant people • understanding roles and responsibilies	

Source: Telephone interviews in Phase One of the NFER study, 2000.

Summary

Benefits

By way of a summary, with regard to the benefits of multi-agency working the following points emerged:

- A large number of benefits to the professionals involved in multi-agency working were highlighted by interviewees, including improved understanding of the roles and responsibilities of different agencies, improved communication and information sharing, better working relationships and the opportunity to discuss and therefore address issues between agencies.

- Interviewees also identified more strategic-level benefits, such as the support that multi-agency working provided for the process of inclusion, improved access to funding and the knock-on effect that a piece of joint working might have for other areas of work.

- Both indirect and direct benefits for the target group of pupils were also identified. A coordinated and holistic approach and one point of access to services, for example, were raised, as well as individual support for pupils and raised achievement.

- Some benefits were apparent regardless of the agencies involved, such as improved understanding of the roles and responsibilities of agencies, joint ownership and a holistic approach to problems, whilst others featured mainly in the work between Social Services and Education, e.g. raised awareness of the needs of the target group, or Health and Education, e.g. the access to specialist expertise gained by schools.

- Whilst often the main benefits associated with different target groups were specific to that group, e.g. raised awareness in the case of LAC, other benefits featured across the target groups, particularly where pupils were targeted directly. In the case of disaffected pupils and children with mental health problems, for example, the fact that their needs were addressed more appropriately through multi-agency working was often raised.

Challenges

The following points emerged in relation to the challenges associated with multi-agency work:

- Overwhelmingly, interviewees identified funding and resource issues as the major challenge for the implementation of multi-agency initiatives. Mentioned in particular were difficulties in sustaining initiatives once the funding ceased and ensuring equity of funding from all partner agencies. Joined-up budgets were suggested as one way to alleviate the latter problem.

- The next most frequently mentioned challenge, although only highlighted by just over one in ten interviewees (14 per cent) compared with just under a third (32 per cent) who referred to funding and resource issues, was time. The time commitment required for setting up initiatives and the subsequent work involved in their implementation were highlighted, as was the time needed to develop relationships with other agencies which, although difficult to find, was felt to be worthwhile in terms of future time savings and improved working practices.

- A range of other challenges was mentioned, although by one in ten or less of interviewees. These included differences between the agencies in terms of priorities, structures, ways of working, and in cultures or perspectives; the difficulty of getting schools, parents and other agencies on board; and problems with information sharing, especially where IT systems were not compatible.

- Some challenges were felt to impact on multi-agency initiatives regardless of which agency was involved, most notably funding and resources, but also time and different approaches or ways of working.

- Other challenges were felt to affect joint working most when all three agencies were involved, for example the need to clarify issues and/or definitions, overcoming professional boundaries, the effect of Government legislation or initiatives, and personnel changes.

- Challenges raised for initiatives where only Social Services and Education were involved included the problem of different timescales and planning cycles and involving Health. Challenges highlighted within initiatives involving only Health and Education included clarifying roles and responsibilities, competing priorities or demands, recruitment issues, and demand.

- Funding or resource issues were highlighted as challenges for initiatives concerning all target groups except those focused on disaffected pupils and children in need or at risk. Challenges for both of these initiatives were most notably time, but also getting others on board, particularly schools in the case of disaffected pupils.

- Interestingly, a challenge identified for multi-agency work with an early years focus was professional readjustment. There was believed to be a need for agencies to take the work more seriously, perhaps echoed in the difficulty highlighted by some interviewees of involving Health.

- Apart from funding, challenges associated with work with pupils with complex needs focused notably on the very complexity of the issues involved, which sometimes could be exacerbated by different agency regulations and legal requirements. At the same time, schools and parents often had very different agendas.

Key factors in success

In summary, the following points were noted with regard to the key factors required for multi-agency work to be successful:

- Commitment from those involved was overwhelmingly nominated as the key factor for successful multi-agency working, with the need for good working relationships raised as the second most important factor. According to interviewees, both factors were considered vital regardless of the agencies involved or the target group or focus of the work.

- Having a person to lead or drive the initiative forward and having a clear focus for multi-agency work, shared aims and shared funding or resources were also considered essential features by many interviewees, with leadership and drive and joint funding being highlighted as particularly important where all three agencies were involved.

- Having a clear focus for the work and joint ownership were nominated more frequently where initiatives involved Social Services and Education, whilst having common aims and the relevant professionals involved were key factors that interviewees associated mainly where joint work was undertaken between Health and Education.

49

♦ Some key factors were identified as particularly relevant for multi-agency work focused on specific target groups or areas, for example the importance of regular and professional meetings for strategic planning was raised, and the importance of spending time on the groundwork where work focused on the needs of children with speech and language difficulties was also highlighted.

FINAL COMMENT

51

The diverse and complex nature of multi-agency activity was evident from the findings of Phase One of the research. Interagency activity focused on a range of target groups and areas of work. The importance of this in determining the rationale for a coordinated approach and the agencies that were involved was also evident.

The value of a multi-agency approach for the professionals involved, as well as the benefits in terms of the outcomes for the target group, were highlighted. However, a number of challenges associated with interagency work were also raised and, in many cases, these factors were also considered to be the key ones considered essential for successful and effective coordination and collaboration.

Phases Two and Three of the research will examine some of the issues touched on in this report in more depth. This will include:

♦ examination of the demarcation of roles and responsibilities of the different agencies engaged in a coordinated approach within different initiatives

♦ ways in which the challenges identified within a specific initiative have been overcome

♦ the skills required by professionals to work successfully and effectively in a multi-agency way

♦ the impact of a multi-agency approach when focused on different target groups and different areas of work.

APPENDICES

Appendix 1. LEA sample information

The types of LEAs in the telephone sample

Table A.1 below shows the breakdown of LEAs nationally by type as a percentage of the overall total, and, similarly, the breakdown of LEAs in the telephone sample by type as a percentage of their overall total. Eight types of LEA were identified as follows:

*   London Boroughs
*   Metropolitan LEAs
*   New authorities with a single city focus
*   New authorities with a regional focus
*   County LEAs
*   Welsh LEAs
*   Northern Ireland Education and Library Boards
*   Island LEAs.

Table A.1   The types of LEA nationally and in the telephone sample

Type of LEA	National		Telephone sample	
	(N)	%	(N)	%
London	33	18	21	18
Metropolitan	37	21	21	18
New regional	31	17	18	15
New city	34	19	23	20
County	15	8	13	11
Welsh	22	12	17	15
Northern Ireland	5	3	2	2
Island	3	2	2	2
Total	**180**	**100**	**117**	**100**

All percentages have been rounded to the nearest whole number, and therefore may not add up to 100.
Source: NFER Database.

Table A.1 shows that the percentage of London and island LEAs were the same as the national average, whilst the percentages of new LEAs with a single city focus and Northern Island Education and Library Boards were also within one per cent of the national average. The percentages of new LEAs with a regional focus and metropolitan authorities were slightly lower than the national average, whilst the percentages of Welsh and county authorities were slightly higher than the national average. Overall, the sample can be considered to reflect the national picture in terms of the types of LEAs represented.

The sizes of the LEAs in the telephone sample

Table A.2 shows how far the telephone sample was representative of the sizes of the LEAs nationally. The size of the LEA was characterised by the number of schools of all types in the LEA (taken from the NFER Schools' Database), which was then broken down into three categories. The full list of 180 LEAs was broken into three equal groups, according to the number of schools in each – thus categories were developed where:

- 1 to 73 schools would constitute a 'small' LEA

- 74 to 116 schools would constitute a 'medium-sized' LEA

- 117 schools and above would constitute a 'large' LEA.

Table A.2   The sizes of LEAs nationally and in the telephone sample

Type of LEA	National		Telephone sample	
	(N)	**%**	**(N)**	**%**
Small	60	33	26	22
Medium	60	33	41	35
Large	60	33	48	41
No data	0	0	2	2
Total	**180**	**100**	**117**	**100**

All percentages have been rounded to the nearest whole number, and therefore may not add up to 100 per cent.
Source: NFER Schools Database.

Table A.2 shows that the percentages of large LEAs and medium-sized LEAs were slightly higher than the national average (by eight per cent and two per cent respectively), whilst the percentage of small LEAs was lower (by 11 per cent) than was the case nationally. Overall, however, a comparison of percentages demonstrates that the sample in this study is representative, in terms of the sizes of LEAs nationally.

Appendix 2. Glossary

Bookstart

Bookstart is a scheme being introduced region by region by Sainsbury's supermarkets in conjunction with Book Trust – an independent charity.

Sainsbury's Bookstart is a national programme run in conjunction with Book Trust, the independent book charity. By making free books available to every baby in the UK, Bookstart encourages parents to look at books with their children from as early an age as possible.

(http://www.bookstart.co.uk/)

Behaviour Support Plan (BSP)

The Behaviour Support Plan (BSP) is a statement prepared by the LEA detailing the arrangements available, or proposed, in their area for the education of children with behavioural difficulties. The plan is a statutory requirement, to help ensure that there are coherent, comprehensive and well-understood local arrangements for helping schools tackle poor behaviour and discipline problems. The plans offer an opportunity to identify where aspects of current provision work well and to facilitate the spread of good practice.

(http://www.dfee.gov.uk/a-z/BEHAVIOUR%5FSUPPORT%5FPLAN_ba.html)

Children's Services Plan (CSP)

Local authorities are required to produce Children's Services Plans outlining their intentions for services for children and young people. The Children's Services Plans of various authorities can often be found on local authority websites.

Connexions

A Government strategy intended to be a single, coherent strategy for all young people.

(http://www.connexions.gov.uk/)

Education Development Plan (EDP)

Documents to be written by local authorities outlining future plans for education in their area.

A well-structured, effective development process will help ensure a coherent strategy to raise standards based on a shared agenda with schools and other partners.

The plan must be sharply focused on raising standards and improving school effectiveness, although it will need to take account of the LEA's wider responsibilities, for example planning school places and ensuring pupil attendance.

(http://www.dfee.gov.uk/edp/edpnet/)

Early Years Development and Childcare Partnership (EYDCP)

The DfEE launched the National Childcare Strategy Green Paper Meeting the Childcare Challenge *in May 1998. It proposed that plans for establishing and developing early years and childcare services should be drawn up and implemented at local level by Early Years Development and Childcare Partnerships.*

(http://www.dfee.gov.uk/eydcp/index.htm)

Health Advisory Service model (HAS model)

A four-tier model of service, recently proposed and implemented within Child and Adolescent Mental Health Services. Each tier represents a different level of specialism.

See pages 15–16 in: DEPARTMENT OF HEALTH (1995). *A Handbook of Child and Adolescent Mental Health*. London: HMSO.

Healthy Schools Initiative (HSI)

The Healthy Schools Initiative was launched in May 1998. This was in response to the White Paper Excellence in Schools, *which committed the Government to helping all schools become healthy schools, and the Green Paper* Our Healthier Nation, *which identified schools as a key setting for implementing the Government's health strategy. The Initiative aims to raise the awareness of children, teachers, governors, parents, and the wider community about the opportunities that exist in schools for improving health.*

(http://www.doh.gov.uk/target33/target33.htm#he)

Quality Protects (QP)

The Quality Protects programme is a key part of the Government's wider strategy for tackling social exclusion. It focuses on working with some of the most disadvantaged and vulnerable children in our society: those children looked after by councils in the child protection system; and other children in need.

(http://www.doh.gov.uk/qualityprotects/index.htm)

Standards Fund (SF)

The Standards Fund is a collection of specific grants which enables schools and LEAs to achieve improvement in education standards set out in agreed targets, particularly for literacy, numeracy, social inclusion and GCSE.

(http://www.dfee.gov.uk/a-z/STANDARDS%5FFUND.html)

Sure Start Initiative

A programme for children up to the age of four, preparing them for entry into formal education.

Sure Start is a radical, cross-departmental strategy to improve services for young children and families. It is targeted at children under four and their families in areas of need.

(http://www.dfee.gov.uk/sstart/intro.htm)